DAD'S LIFE

– IN –

HIS WORDS

BY

_____

Questions or feedback about this book?

We'd love to hear from you!

pkppublisher@gmail.com

TABLE OF CONTENTS

DEDICATION
✳ · ✳ · ✳

A Tip For Dad

Use the lines below to write a dedication to the person(s) for whom you are writing this book.

_____

_____

_____

_____

_____

_____

_____

ABOUT THIS BOOK
··*

I personalized this book for:

_____

I presented this book to:

_____

on:

_____
(date or occasion)

GETTING STARTED
�֎ · �֎ · �֎

If you're ready to jump right in and begin completing the pages of this book, that's great—go for it! You might, however, find yourself hesitant or unsure of how to get started. If so, we've got your back!

We've included several special resources at the back of the book to help you "get out of your own way" and maximize the value you and your loved ones will get out of the book.

Go to page 97 and begin with reading "How To Use This Book." Continue with "A Special Message for Dad" on page 99, and the pages following. There you will find guidance to assist you with opening your mind and imagination, and in breaking through any barriers that might be holding you back from getting started.

Revisit those pages as often as needed.

DAD'S ORIGIN STORY

BIRTH
✳ · ✳ · ✳

I was born on the _____ of _____
           (day)   (month)

in the year _____.
           (year)

I was born in _____
                        (country / city / state)

                              at

_____
        (location, e.g., name of hospital, at home, etc.)

I was given the name:

_____

I was named after or my name has the following special meaning:

_____

I was number _____ in the birth order.

My parents had _____ children in all.

The names of my siblings are:

_____

_____

_____

_____

_____

_____

_____

My parents names are _____ and

_____.

My grandparents names (mother's side) are

_____ and

_____.

My grandparents names (father's side) are

_____ and

_____.

My father worked as a _____ and

my mother _____.

When I was born _____
                        (name of head of state)

was _____
          (President, Prime Minister, etc.)

of _____.
          (Country)

A significant historical event that took place the year I was born is:

_____

A significant historical event that took place during my childhood

is _____. That happened in the

year _____ on _____.

Other Notes, Thoughts, or Memories. . .

_____

_____

_____

_____

_____

_____

_____

_____

_____

_____

_____

_____

_____

CHILDHOOD (AGE 0—12)
✳ · ✳ · ✳

I grew up in _____.

(city / town)

Something I liked about growing up there was:

_____

_____

_____

I went to school at _____.

My favorite teacher was named _____.

The reason he / she was my favorite was because:

_____

_____

My least favorite teacher was named:

_____.

The reason he / she was my least favorite was because:

_____

_____

My favorite subject at school was _____.

My nickname was _____.

As a child, I thought that when I grew up I would like to be:

_____

I enjoyed the following activities as a child:

_____   _____

_____   _____

_____   _____

_____   _____

One of my favorite childhood memories is:

_____

_____

_____

My family would spend time together in the following ways:

_____

_____

_____

My family had these holiday traditions:

_____

_____

_____

_____

My favorite TV show was _____.

My favorite toy was _____.

I was expected to do the following chores:

_____

_____

One of my best friends growing up was named:

_____.

I enjoyed _____ with _____.

Someone who served as a special mentor to me was:

_____.

From this person, I learned:

_____

_____

_____

When I thought about my future, I expected it would be:

_____

_____

Other Notes, Thoughts, or Memories. . .

_____

_____

_____

_____

_____

_____

_____

_____

_____

_____

_____

_____

_____

_____

TEENAGE YEARS
✳ · ✳ · ✳

I turned 13 years old on the _____ of _____

in the year _____, and officially became a teenager.

As a teenager, I attended school at _____.

My favorite teacher was named _____.

The reason he / she was my favorite was because:

_____

_____

My least favorite teacher was named:

_____.

The reason he / she was my least favorite was because:

_____

_____

My favorite subject at school during my teenage years was

_____.

As a teenager, I thought that when I grew up I would like to be:

_____

I enjoyed the following activities as a teenager:

_____   _____

_____   _____

_____   _____

_____   _____

One of my favorite teenage memories is:

_____

_____

_____

My favorite food as a teenager was _____.

One of my best friends as a teenager was named

_____.

I enjoyed _____ with _____.

Someone who served as a special mentor to me during my teenage years was:

_____.

From this person, I learned:

_____

_____

_____

As a teenager, I got my first job as _____

at _____.

My rate of pay was _____.

I got in trouble when I:

_____

_____

As a teenager, I thought my parents were _____.

However, as an adult looking back, I realize:

_____

_____

When I was a teenager and thought about my future, I expected:

_____

_____

_____

Other Notes, Thoughts, or Memories. . .

_____

_____

_____

_____

_____

_____

_____

_____

_____

_____

_____

_____

_____

YOUNG ADULTHOOD
✳ · ✳ · ✳

When I finished school at age _____, I decided that I would

_____.

Other jobs I worked after my schooling included:

_____   _____

_____   _____

_____   _____

_____   _____

I met my wife, _____, at

_____.

Here's how we met:

_____

_____

_____

When I first met her, I thought she was _____.

And she thought I was _____.

For our first date, we _____.

When we were dating, we used to enjoy doing the following activities or going to the following places together:

_____   _____

_____   _____

_____   _____

_____   _____

We dated for _____ (months / years) before we were married.

We were married on _____.

Our wedding ceremony was at _____.

We had our reception at _____.

Our Best Man was _____ and our

Maid/Matron of Honor was _____.

We went on a honeymoon to _____.

A special memory about our wedding day is:

_____

_____

_____

_____

After we were married, we lived in a _____
                                        (house, condo, apartment)

in _____.
            (town / city)

One way that life changed after we were married was:

_____

_____

_____

Something that I learned about how to be a good husband is:

_____

_____

_____

Other Notes, Thoughts, or Memories. . .

MARRIED LIFE & STARTING A FAMILY
✳ · ✳ · ✳

After I married, I was working as a _____

at _____,

while Mom _____.

Something I remember vividly about those early married years is:

_____

_____

_____

After we were married, _____ did the cooking.

My favorite meal was _____.

We had our first child, _____, on

_____.

Our other children include:

_____

_____

_____

_____

_____

_____

Here are some memories of each of my children:

_____

_____

_____

_____

_____

_____

_____

_____

What I found challenging about being a father was:

_____

_____

Something I am grateful for about being a father is:

_____

_____

One way that being a father helped me grow to be a better man:

_____

_____

Other Notes, Thoughts or Memories:

_____

_____

_____

_____

_____

_____

_____

_____

_____

_____

_____

_____

DAD'S LIFE TODAY
✳ · ✳ · ✳

I am currently working / not working / retired. (circle)

My current job is _____.

What keeps me busy is _____.

What I like about my current / last job is:

_____

What I didn't like about my current / last job is:

_____

Some of my closest friends today include:

_____

_____

_____

_____

_____

One of my favorite things to do today is:

_____

If I could go on vacation anywhere, it would be to:

_____

with _____

Generally, the best part of my day is:

_____

And the best part of my week is usually:

_____

_____

(activity engaged in, or place you go)

Other Notes, Thoughts, or Memories. . .

_____

_____

_____

_____

_____

_____

_____

_____

_____

_____

_____

_____

_____

DAD'S FAVORITE THINGS
✳ · ✳ · ✳

My favorite type of music is _____.

My favorite song is _____

by_____.

My favorite sport is _____, and my

favorite team / athlete is _____.

My favorite movie is _____.

My favorite TV show is _____.

My favorite thing to do as a family is:

_____.

My favorite book or story is _____.

My favorite joke is:

_____

_____

_____

_____

My favorite family memory:

_____

_____

My favorite family vacation:

_____

My favorite meal is _____.

My favorite beverage is _____.

My favorite dessert is _____.

My favorite restaurant is _____.

My favorite recipe is:

_____

_____

_____

_____

_____

_____

_____

_____

My favorite place I've ever visited:

_____

Other Notes, Thoughts, or Memories. . .

_____

_____

_____

_____

_____

_____

_____

_____

_____

_____

_____

_____

SIGNIFICANT EVENTS THAT HAPPENED IN DAD'S LIFETIME

HISTORICAL EVENTS
※ · ※ · ※

Here are some significant historical (world / national) events that happened during my lifetime:

EVENT	WHEN

The historical event that I will always most remember is:

_____

_____

It had the following impact on me:

_____

_____

_____

_____

_____

_____

_____

_____

_____

_____

PERSONAL EVENTS
✳ · ✳ · ✳

Here are some significant events that happened during my life that helped me to become the person I am today:

EVENT	WHEN
_____	_____
_____	_____
_____	_____
_____	_____
_____	_____
_____	_____
_____	_____

The personal event that I will always most remember is:

_____

_____

It had the following impact on me:

_____

_____

_____

_____

_____

_____

_____

_____

_____

DAD'S DREAMS, GOALS, THOUGHTS, & WISDOM

DAD'S DREAMS & GOALS
* · * · *

If I could live anywhere in the world, it would be:

_____

If I could visit anywhere in the world, I would go to:

_____

Some achievements that I'm proud to have accomplished include:

_____

_____

_____

_____

_____

A goal I am currently working on is:

_____

Something I'd love to learn (about, or how to do) is:

_____

Someone I greatly admire is_____,

and the reason is:

_____

_____

Other Notes, Thoughts, or Memories. . .

_____

_____

_____

_____

_____

_____

_____

_____

_____

_____

_____

_____

_____

_____

WISDOM FROM DAD
✳ · ✳ · ✳

Something I have learned about effectively dealing with people is:

_____

_____

_____

_____

_____

I believe the most important quality to be successful is:

_____

_____

_____

_____

Here's how I approach difficult decisions:

_____

_____

_____

_____

One thing I want my loved ones reading this book to know about life is:

_____

_____

_____

_____

_____

_____

If I could teach the world one thing, it would be:

_____

_____

_____

_____

_____

A big challenge I overcame was:

_____

_____

_____

_____

_____

And the lesson I learned from that struggle was:

_____

_____

_____

_____

_____

_____

An important lesson I learned from my family is:

_____

_____

_____

_____

_____

_____

I believe I have gained most of my wisdom from:

_____

_____

_____

_____

_____

If I could go back and do something differently in life, it would be:

_____

_____

_____

_____

_____

_____

_____

Other Notes, Thoughts, or Memories. . .

_____

_____

_____

_____

_____

_____

_____

_____

_____

_____

_____

_____

FINAL THOUGHTS FROM DAD
✳ · ✳ · ✳

Something I want my loved ones reading this book to always remember:

_____

_____

_____

_____

_____

_____

_____

_____

_____

_____

What I hope my family will always remember about me is:

_____

_____

_____

_____

_____

_____

_____

_____

_____

_____

_____

I hope my children will always remember this about their mother:

_____

_____

_____

_____

_____

_____

_____

_____

_____

_____

_____

_____

And something important to remember about your siblings is:

_____

_____

_____

_____

_____

_____

_____

_____

_____

_____

_____

_____

If you focus on the following, you will undoubtedly live a good life:

_____

_____

_____

_____

_____

_____

_____

_____

_____

_____

_____

_____

Other Final Thoughts From Dad. . .

_____

_____

_____

_____

_____

_____

_____

_____

_____

_____

_____

_____

_____

PHOTOGRAPHS, ETC.

A Tip For Dad

We've provided the following pages to allow room for you to optionally include any special photographs, newspaper clippings, etc. You can use a glue stick or tape to secure them.

LINED PAGES

A Tip For Dad

Use the following lined pages for notes, drafts, as additional space for sharing other stories or even to write a letter to your loved ones.

HELPFUL RESOURCES

HOW TO USE THIS BOOK
∗ · ∗ · ∗

If you are holding this book in your hands, you most likely fit into one of four categories:

1. You are planning to give this book to a father, so he can personalize it for his child or children.

2. You may be Dad, and you bought this book to personalize it for your child or children.

3. Someone gave you this book and invited you to personalize it for your child or children.

4. Or, you may have received this book (already personalized) as a gift from your father.

If you fall into the first category (1), please encourage Dad to read this "How To Use This Book" section, as it will help explain the purpose of the book, and provide a sense of why it will mean so much to have him personalize it.

If you fall in the last category above (4), you are truly blessed! We hope you will cherish this book forever as a special memento, and share it with other loved ones over the years, to help them appreciate the man you call "Dad."

If you are in one of the two middle categories above (2 or 3; you've either bought the book to personalize it and pass it on to your child / children; or you were given the book with a request to personalize it), <u>the next section of the book is primarily for you.</u>

In the next few pages, we want to offer encouragement and suggestions, so that this book will enrich the lives of everyone involved, and perhaps even live on as a family heirloom for generations to come! So turn the page, and keep reading…

A SPECIAL MESSAGE FOR DAD
✳ · ✳ · ✳

Upon receiving this book and flipping through the pages, you might find yourself feeling at least slightly overwhelmed. It might look like "work" to you. If you've been given this book as a "gift," you might feel a bit like now you have had this expectation put on you to complete something and give it back to the person. *(When did I agree to do this?)* You might be concerned about the time it will take. Or maybe you've looked at some of the questions, and found one or more that you're pretty sure you can't answer.

If some variation of the above paragraph describes the way you're feeling, we want to assure you that wherever you are at, *it's perfectly okay*. And secondly, we want to invite you to relax. It's going to be ok. *Promise!*

We'll get to some of the practical considerations in a moment. But for now, please take a moment to realize that this book *really is* a gift. In fact, it's a reflection of the gift of the relationship that you have with the person for whom you are invited to complete this book. It's a gift for you to know that you are loved and valued, and loved and valued so much that someone wants, or will want, to read a book all about you. And that they will read it with the same fascination and attention that one might read an autobiography of a powerful world leader, a revered athlete or artist, an inventor, business tycoon, or change maker. You are truly *that* important in the eyes of the person for whom you are going to complete this book.

We suggest that you'll find the process of reflecting on your life, your experiences, and what you've learned in your short time on the planet an enriching exercise. It may stir up some difficult moments and memories, and surely will stir up some great ones as well.

It's a gift to know or discover that someone wants to know about your life, your experiences, your thoughts, your likes and dislikes, your history, and so on. And it will be an incredible gift to them once you've poured yourself out on paper and passed the completed book to them. If you aren't sure about that, trust us!

FIVE PRINCIPLES TO GUIDE YOU
✳ · ✳ · ✳

Here are five suggested Guiding Principles that we recommend you keep in mind as you start out on the journey of personalizing this book.

Principle 1:
This Is YOUR Book

This book will be created by *you*. And this book is for *your* loved ones.

We truly want you to recognize this book as your own, and make it so. You may find there are questions within that do not apply to you, or that you do not want to answer for one reason or another. Feel free to leave them blank, or even cross them out entirely! Feel free to write a snarky comment next to it about why you don't like the question!

You may find some questions are close to being relevant, but they are worded in a way that just doesn't quite fit your life, situation, or relationship. Feel free to re-write the question. Scribble out the words that don't fit, and replace them with words that **do** reflect your situation. Perhaps you've had the experience of giving or receiving a greeting card that was "almost perfect," and was corrected to customize it to the situation or relationship (such as changing an "I" to a "We"). That's what we're after here. Those customizations actually enhance the meaningfulness of the card, as they inject something personal and unique into the message. That is your opportunity anytime you find a question that doesn't fit.

We've also intentionally left blank space throughout. You have our permission to write all over the page as you see fit. Feel free to include little drawings or doodles if you choose. You can add further explanations or anecdotes wherever you want. Add in the little details that occur to you—that the pre-written questions just don't cover.

Principle 2:
Commit To Completion

We invite you to commit to complete this book, and do it as soon as you can (within reason). We've created it to be **simple**, **quick** and **fun** to complete (even for those who think they aren't very good writers). And it will provide tremendous value for your loved ones once it's completed.

A word about the word "completion."

"Completion" of this book does not necessarily mean you've filled in every single "blank" or answered every question.

It means simply getting the book finished, however that looks to you, and then passing it to the person or people you completed it for.

Remember, this is YOUR book. (Remember that previous principle?). So you even get to decide what "complete" looks like!

Principle 3:
"Done" Is Better Than "Perfect"

If you struggle with perfectionism, you may feel a hesitation to even begin, or maybe you'll begin, and then feel tempted to stop. You may have been raised with the idea that if something is worth doing, it's worth doing right. We'd like to counter that with the following:

If something is worth doing, do it.

Simple, right?

It may be easier to say than to practice. But really, forget about the perfect rendition of this book, in which every question is answered with perfect accuracy and completeness. That version of the book does not actually exist, except in your mind. And the book in your mind will never make it into the hands of your loved one(s). The only one that actually *will* make it into their hands is the one in your hands. The one you are reading now. And the path to getting it to them is actually **doing it**.

As the saying goes, *perfect is the enemy of the good.*

In fact, we believe so strongly that you must reject the pursuit of perfection in taking on this project that we've included a "Page To Intentionally Mess Up," so that you can destroy the illusion of perfection right from the start.

If you're still struggling with this, the next point may help loosen things for you a bit more.

Principle 4:
Rather Than "Biography"...Think "Snapshot"

What do you think of when you hear the word *snapshot*? Probably the camera going *click!* and produces a photograph capturing a moment in time. A single moment. A snapshot may be carefully framed, or the button may have been hastily pressed, and the lens may not have even been fully focused. Either way, you get a snapshot.

When you think of of a Biography, you might think of research. You might think of facts and figures, confirming through multiple sources, and citations. You might think of the importance of precision, or at least a strained attempt at achieving it.

Although this book is a book and not a photograph, we suggest that it's actually much more like a snapshot than a biography.

A snapshot doesn't tell the totality of a person's life. It captures an image at a moment in time. It doesn't tell the whole story, always and forever. And yet, a photograph can still have immense value.

Loved ones don't value an "old" photograph any less just because the person in the picture has changed in appearance. The photograph is a cherished snapshot of the person at the time it was taken. It's similar with this book. You're capturing your thoughts as they occur to you at the moment the snapshot is taken. Your thoughts, opinions, and even memories and recollections may change over time. And that's okay.

Let's apply what we've been discussing to actually working on the book. Let's say you come across a question that you might be tempted to "sit on" for a long time and ponder. That is one way to go about it. However, we suggest you go with your gut. Don't allow questions asking for your "favorite" this, or "best" that, or "most cherished" whatever cause you to delay until you are certain you have the absolute answer. Sure, pause a moment to think, but, then give your response. It might help to imagine you are being interviewed on television, or are a contestant on a gameshow, and you have to give your answer because the show host and the audience are waiting. What would you say? Now say that. Get it on paper. (Because, after all, "done is better than perfect." Always.)

Should you ever reach the point that you realize you have many NEW answers, and that, like an old photograph, the old ones hardly even look like you anymore, you can always order another copy and go through the exercise again! We know your loved ones would be thrilled to receive another copy of a completely different version of the "same" book.

Principle 5:
Share Yourself Freely

This book offers a true opportunity to express yourself. To pour yourself out on paper.

One of the greatest pleasures we can have in life is sharing with other people. Share your life and memories and thoughts with your loved ones. Put it all out there, sharing generously.

We recommend you consider completing the book and gifting it to your loved one as soon as possible. You might be tempted to stash it away in a "legacy drawer" or safe deposit box or the like. While it will definitely have great meaning to your loved ones upon your eventual passing, we suggest it could have even more value now, while you are alive and (hopefully!) well. You might find that sharing with your loved ones will allow for a beautiful dialogue to take place. They may ask you follow-up questions that will allow for more sharing. And they may share with you things that you never knew about them, perhaps including just how much the completed book means to them.

A final thought

It's been said that the greatest obstacle standing between most aspiring writers and their completed book is the *lack of a fixed deadline*. Without a deadline, the manuscript exists only as a vague hope for someday. With a deadline, writers get into action, and books get written.

The same is true with this book here. We suggest setting a deadline for yourself. You can choose to approach it either based on a particular date by which you'll complete the book (e.g., by March 15th), or by allocating a certain amount of time to its completion (e.g., 2 hours). You might find that setting a timer and working for even 5, 10, or 15 minutes at a time, you can make a lot of progress over several short blocks.

Please revisit these suggested principles as often as necessary. You may find that even a brief glance at this section of the book each time you sit down to work on it proves helpful.

Wishing you and your loved ones many blessings from your taking on and completing this project!

A FINAL NOTE
✳ · ✳ · ✳

If the above guidance sounds like it was written precisely for you, and you related to the concerns and hangups expressed, it's no coincidence. We (the husband and wife team who started Personalized Keepsake Publishing) have struggled against the very tendencies expressed here in various ways, in both our personal and professional lives. We get it!

You can take comfort in knowing that we don't just preach this advice—we strive to live it. In fact, we resisted our own perfectionist tendencies and harnessed the power of deadlines to ensure this book actually landed in your hands. Are there some things that could be improved in the book? No doubt. But "done" is better than "perfect"—all the time.

We invite you to push beyond whatever might potentially thwart you from completing this book so you can bring it to the person(s) you love. It will mean the world to them. And that's what this book is all about.

By the way...

It's entirely possible that this "How To Use This Book" section may strike you as over-the-top, or even completely ridiculous and unnecessary. You might be wondering what all the fuss is about. And maybe you've even already completed the book and are just circling back now, skimming over this section for the first time. If that is you: good work! And know that the rest of us envy you! :)

PAGE TO INTENTIONALLY MESS UP
✳ · ✳ · ✳

If you are concerned about making this book perfect, we want to help you break free of that. Use the space below to intentionally "mess up" the book. Scribble on the page. Draw an ugly mark. Intentionally spill some coffee or tea on the pages. Mess it up now to remind yourself you aren't after perfection--you're after sharing yourself on the page with your loved one(s).

Your act of intentional imperfection is an act of service—to yourself, and to those who will benefit from this book once it's completed. *So go ahead and mess it up!*

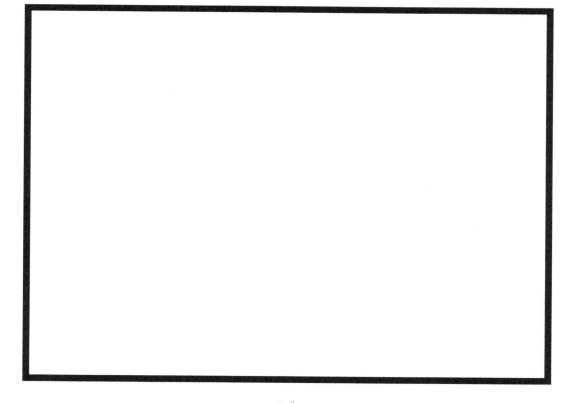